PUSH

Manifesting Your God-Given Potential

Latrivette Williams

ISBN 978-1-64515-561-4 (paperback)
ISBN 978-1-64515-562-1 (digital)

Copyright © 2019 by Latrivette Williams

All rights reserved. No part of this publication may be reproduced, distributed, or transmitted in any form or by any means, including photocopying, recording, or other electronic or mechanical methods without the prior written permission of the publisher. For permission requests, solicit the publisher via the address below.

Christian Faith Publishing, Inc.
832 Park Avenue
Meadville, PA 16335
www.christianfaithpublishing.com

Printed in the United States of America

All scriptures contained within this book are referenced from one of these sources, some are marked by abbreviation of translation and some are not:

Mirror Bible: The Bible translated from the original text and paraphrased in contemporary speech with commentary. Copyright © 2012 by Francois du Toit. All rights reserved.

New Living Translation: Scriptures are taken from the Holy Bible, New Living Translation, copyright © 1996, 2004, 2007, Tyndale House Publishers, Inc.

New International Version: NIV Compact Thinline Bible, Copyright © 2006 by Zondervan. The Holy Bible, *New International Version* Copyright © 1973, 1978, 1984 by Biblica, Inc. All rights reserved.

King James Bible: In The KJV Reference Bible: Compact Edition, Hendrickson Publishers conforms its setting of the King James or Authorized Version to its most highly regarded edition: *The Cambridge Paragraph Bible* of 1873, edited by F. H. A. Scrivener

Modern English Version: The Kenneth Copeland Word of Faith Study Bible, copyright © 2017 by Kenneth Copeland. The Holy Bible, Modern English Version Copyright © 2014 by Military Bible Association. All rights reserved.

The Living Bible: *The Living Bible* Copyright © 1971 owned by assignment by KNT Charitable Trust. All rights reserved. Verses marked TLB are taken from *The Living Bible,* copyright 1971. Used by permission of Tyndale House Publishers, Inc., Wheaton, Illinois 60189. All rights reserved.

The Message Translation and The Amplified Version Bible was taken from Bible Gateway: www.biblegateway.com, seller HarperCollins Christian Publishing, Inc.

All quotes that are used throughout this book comes from these sources and by the author herself, Latrivette Williams.

30 motivational Jim Rohn Quotes that will change your life. Copyright 2017. All rights reserved- Project Life Mastery/Terms of Use/Privacy Policy/Affiliate Disclosure.

Sushan Sharma copyright © 2017 searchquotes.com and/or its licensors. All rights reserved.

I dedicate this book to my daughter ShaCorie Cockrell and step-children, Kiyana Williams and Andre Williams Jr. May this inspire you to be your best self and live your best life.

Contents

Introduction 9

Chapter 1: Every Day Is a New Day 11
              Make it a great day or not 17
              Own Your Choices 19
              Should I Follow My Heart? 22

Chapter 2: Who Are You Waiting On? 26
              You Think You Have Forever 29
              God Cares! 32
              Be Mindful With Whom You Share 36

Chapter 3: When Things Get Hard, You Mustn't Quit ...38
              The Word of God is Practical 41
              Biblical Principles Work 43
              This Too Shall Pass 46

Chapter 4: Love: The Essence of Life 49
              The Principle of Sowing and Reaping 52
              Patience Perfect Work 54
              The Peace of Praise 57

Introduction

When I observed my life and saw the position I was in verses where I longed to be, I knew that I wasn't living my best life. The mind-blowing thing about my situation was that, I wasn't where I was because I had to be or because I couldn't do better, I was where I was in life as a result of my choices and my ignorance to change them. I would read and study about the abundant life that God has provided for us, but I wasn't living it. I would allow temporary defeat to get the best of me and blur my vision from the truth; the truth of who I am in Christ and about what his word say I can do. I was a coward. I coward away from opportunities, people, and my true self. I walked with my head held high and spoke very boldly, but the truth was, when times came for me to express and expand myself I was afraid and I retreated. I would tell myself: What if I'm not good enough? What will people say? What if I'm wrong? And because of the negative advice I gave myself, I wasn't seeing the results I desired. Because of my negative view of self, I wasn't releasing my gifts to the world, or being true to my being. But one day, I decided to act on my instincts to push. To push beyond my self-sabotaging negative advice, fears, behaviors, and doubts. And boy did this decision change my life, I'm sorry it's changing my life. Looking back, I'm so glad I made that decision. Although it was out of my comfort zone, it was so liberating. How about you? Have you ever responded to life like this? Have you ever coward away from something you wanted badly? Have you ever said you'll wait until things get better before you make your move? If you answered yes to these questions, know that it's not too late to make a change. In fact, you picked up this book because you desire to manifest your God-given potential, despite your previous actions. Here's the thing, the only person that can change your life is you, you must decide that you're ready to move forward and then actually begin moving forward. I decided that I was going to transform my life, so that I could live my best life. So I'm encouraging you to Push. Push beyond criticism, doubt, worry and fear and begin today, being your best self and living your best life.

Chapter 1

Every Day Is a New Day

*"Your Life does not get better by chance.
It gets better by change." Jim Rohn*

Carpe diem! *YESTERDAY* has passed, *TODAY* is your present, *TOMORROW* will take care of itself. Have you ever paid attention to just how much of your day is consumed by your thoughts about the past and about the future? All throughout the day we are back and forth with past and future events. In doing this, we don't realize how much of our day we miss. Unfortunately, the clock doesn't stop ticking as we venture off into our past for hours, or spend countless minutes anxiously anticipating every waking moment of our future. Instead, we presently miss out on precious present moments because we are rarely present. Nothing we do today can change our past and the future is not yet revealed. The only thing we have is *Today*. The seeds we plant today will be the harvest we reap later. For this reason, Matthew 6:34 states, "So do not worry about tomorrow; for tomorrow will care for itself." When you take care of today, you are inevitably taking care of your tomorrow. Enjoy the gift of life, today. Allow the beauties and the opportunities of today to take your breath away. Don't take today for granted. Every day is essential and every day is essential for the success of our goals. To keep from taking the day for granted and to fully take advantage of it, you must take advantage of your mornings. Your mornings are the best part of your day, they're fresh and signifies new beginnings and opportunities. If we start our day on a good note, we are more than likely to end our day on a good note. If we start our day on a bad note, we are more than likely to end our day on a bad note. It has been said that the first thirty minutes to an hour are the most important part of our day. These are the moments we are very impressionable and are normally open to a fresh start. Within those thirty minutes to an hour, we are setting the intentions for our day. Whether we want to achieve some goal or scratch something off the bucket list, we are preparing ourselves for the day. Because our thoughts and feelings direct our actions, the things we set our hearts towards first thing in the morning are normally the things that drives our day. If you notice your mood being less than pleasant first thing in the morning, become aware of your thoughts and change them by becoming more optimistic about the situation, or circumstance. If you don't redirect your thoughts, by the time you have your first cup of coffee you would have rehearsed the entire dilemma many times over making the situation much bigger than it has to be and at the same time making yourself one unhappy camper. I suggest you not soak over the mishaps of your past or become weary by worrying about your future. Each day is so precious and unique you don't want to rob it of its potential. Pining over spilled milk, or living in fear over your future will rob you of motivation, inspiration, and application. If you've been quite the Debbie downer, always hard on yourself concerning your past, or anxious over your future, manage your emotions and Carpe Diem.

God has given us the world to enjoy, it's to our shame if we aren't enjoying it. Looking back, I wasn't enjoying life. I was unhappy with my weight. Unhappy with my job. Stressed out over parenting. Struggling in my marriage. Unhappy with where I was in life. I was waking up every day, but every day didn't feel like a fresh start. I didn't seize the opportunities that were staring me in the face, I limited myself by having such limiting beliefs. Limited in how far I could travel. Limited in my career. Limited with where I could live. Limited in the vehicle I could drive. I had not even begun to tap into the potential of my day or my life. For many years, I lived like that and I would have continued to go down that path had I not begun taking the limits off. When we fail to take advantage of the bounties of each day, we cheat ourselves and fail to express untapped potential within. I wasn't taking advantage of my days or taking charge of my mornings. I wasn't redirecting my thoughts because I didn't know I had to. Each day wasn't much different from the other. Just about every day carried the same routine, outlook, drive, and attitude. In fact, if someone had asked me in my early twenties what my passion in life is, I couldn't have told them. Growing up, I didn't envision myself being an author or having my own business or teaching the word of God. By my mid-twenties things began to change. I was coming into an awareness of my purpose by this great desire and excitement to understand mind and behavior. Having this awareness of purpose gave me direction. For the first time I felt my life had meaning. To fully embrace this new lease on life, I knew that it was not enough to know my path, knowing was only half the equation, walking it out would be the other half. I was very excited about embracing purpose, but I wasn't aware of the mental reconditioning it would take for me to live in purpose. I enrolled in school, but I battled with the idea of quitting, often. I wasn't focused at times as I needed to be. I wasn't consistent with studying, class participation, and being mentally focused. As a result of not being consistent with my positive action steps, I failed a course or two. I accumulated a debt that I couldn't pay. A few months before completion I was dismissed from school until I could bring my account to zero balance. There I was: having discovered my purpose, enrolled in school, then upon approaching completion I was faced with the consequences to my actions. In all honesty, being dismissed was a bit of relief for me. I felt like for once, I didn't have to choose between school, or no school and that the decision had been made for me. As you can tell, I really wasn't aware of mind renewal at that time. Neither had I given much notice to cause and effect. I was however, in the mist of it all, still sure of the calling that was and is on my life. Not fully understanding the path I was now on didn't give me any reason to throw the towel in. I knew that I was embarking upon something that was great, at least I knew it felt great. Even if it took a few wrong turns to make the right turn I was determined to see where my passion would take me. Sometimes when things become challenging as they sometimes will, we have a habit of submitting to our conditions; but not me, not that time. Although things were going wrong, I didn't continue to go with it. By being optimistic, I was able to see other ways of pursuing my dreams. Things started looking up for me. I didn't allow my challenges to stop me.

Progress is a process. I continued pursuing my passion in spite of my situation. With much help, I became intentional concerning my purpose and began living life on my terms; being morally conscious of the word of God of course. Through the ongoing process of reconditioning my paradigm daily, I am able to remain focused and I now seize each day. Giving up on my passion in the mist of all odds wasn't an option for me, especially when I took inventory of my life relative to the promises of God and I saw that I was only experiencing very little of our opulent, vast universe. I was no longer satisfied by the mediocrity of my life. Just enough was no longer enough, and I became uncomfortable by my conviction of greatness lying dormant within me. I was no longer okay with just being okay. I was no longer okay with the patterns of my self-sabotaging thought life.

The conviction for more awakened my passion on the inside of me. Being a student of the Bible and believer of the word I knew God's answers to his promises for my life was yes, but what I didn't know at that time was why they weren't manifesting. What were the blocks that was hindering me? I needed answers. I was curious. I wanted to go beyond my norm of just talking about my problems and venting my frustrations. I knew that something was going on beyond my understanding. At that time, I was oblivious to the fact that whatever I was experiencing was what I was subconsciously attracting into my life. I grew up hearing that God was in control of my life and that he was orchestrating my affairs. I came to realize that I am a free will being and that he would never make my decisions for me. However, he is always ready to give himself through infinite wisdom. God has given us every principle we need to live a godly and full life and it's up to us to make the choice to live by them. The Bible instructs us, out of all the information we gather we must get an understanding (see

Proverbs 4:7). Although studying the bible had been a daily habit, I openly admit I still had much to understand especially concerning my life after my spiritual conversion, but one thing that was now crystal clear, I wasn't stuck on damsel in distress street anymore. I was finding out just how relevant Newton's Third Law is to our lives. For our actions always has an equal and opposite reaction. Simple cause and effect. In the Bible it is written that we can either choose the path of life or choose the path of death. God shows us his heart towards us when he said, I desire that you would choose life. God knew what I was now finding out, that the choices we make can be life or death to our circumstances and situations (see Deuteronomy 30:15-20). Prior to understanding what I now know I made the best decisions that I thought was best for my life based upon the knowledge I had at that time. Now I have grown in my understanding, and because I know better I make the effort to do better. I haven't reached a point of perfection by all means, but I'm growing to be a greater version of myself every day. Looking back my life was out of control, I appeared to be in the driver seat but I wasn't. Most of the time I operated out of old conditioning. Even though I read the bible every day, I was reading but not understanding how to apply its wisdom to my life. I attended church, prayed and sought advice from those who are too truth seekers. Eventually little by little I began receiving revelations. Upon the pages of the Bible is all the wisdom we need for every perfect, or imperfect experience in life. There is a scripture in Romans the twelfth chapter the second verse that says, "Do not conform any longer to the pattern of this world, but be transformed by the renewing of your mind. Then you will be able to test and approve what God's will is- his good, pleasing, and perfect will." This was a major life changer for me, I was understanding the importance of renewing my mind. I reasoned: if my unrenewed mindset had gotten me where I was, then what would happen if I began renewing my mind? What would happen if I would respond to life instead of reacting to it? What if I got my hopes up and really expected the best for my life? What if I would make plans that are conducive for my goals and the success of each day? I concluded, that if I continuously renew my mind to God's perfect, good and pleasing will for my life,

I could have the future that God has planned for me. A future of prosperity and hope. I was no longer the victim that I portrayed to be and I knew that God had already perfected everything concerning me, therefore, He had already rescued me in my distress. I was now gaining momentum. I was understanding myself and life more than ever. I took God up on his word and I began putting on the new man, I began to take on a better way of thinking and living my life. Although I knew that habits didn't just go away overnight, I was determined to make a change, besides it's not like I would be on my own, I have the Helper; Holy Spirit to help me. With all the revelation I was getting, I could no longer sell myself short of who I am, or what God has made available. I was enjoying getting to know myself and who he has always known me to be. With a new lease on life, each day has become much more joyful, meaningful, peaceful, and thrilling. I was able to breathe a sigh of relief because I knew my life would be different.

I knew I wasn't helpless. My situation wasn't unique; in fact, the truth about my situation was that the only limitations I was experiencing were the one's I placed upon myself. I needed to believe in me and know that everything that I needed to live a happy fruitful life was already within me. I was affirmed through my believing in the best in me, that is, in Christ. I knew that I was perfect for the purpose. There were absolutely no more excuses for me not to show up for my life. My life was no one else's responsibility, I was responsible for me. I am the manager of my emotions and I control the outcome of my life, the captain of my soul.

Make it a great day or not

"Do what makes you happy!"
Latrivette Williams

You're fast asleep in your warm comfortable bed when the sound of the alarm goes off, beep…beep…beep. There is no other sound that is as annoying as the reoccurring beeping sound in your ear during such early hours of the morning. Your sleep is just now getting really good and you're not quite ready to get up and start your day. So, you snooze the alarm clock until there is only enough time left to jump out of bed head straight for the shower put on your clothes and make it to work with no time to spare. You bob and weave your way through traffic angrily because no one else but you are in a rush. By the time you make it to work, you're catching your breath from all of the running you had to do in order to make it on time. At least that's how it was for me. I hated when my alarm went off at four thirty in the morning for a job that I wasn't in love with. There were mornings I literally wanted to cry because I didn't want to go. When other people would leave the job, I felt sad because I felt like everyone else was moving forward but me. Chances are, you're not hitting the snooze button because you're bubbling with excitement over your life right now. You're stalling to get your day going because it's not ideal. You may be like I was, not liking the condition of your circumstances. When that alarm goes off, all you feel is dread, the dread of doing something, or being someone you have no desire being, or doing. For some people, getting your day started may mean attending events you don't want to attend. It may mean taking care of everyone else but yourself. It may mean staying in a relationship that no longer cultivates growth, or going after a promotion at a job you strongly dislike, all because you feel a since of security. What's so great about each day is that every day we have the opportunity to change the narrative of our lives. If there is one thing I've learned is that, we can change whatever part of our lives we are uncomfortable with if it's within our bounds to change. With wisdom, begin fighting for the things you want. Don't allow yourself to be overcome with fear of change or fear of failure; take a leap of faith. Impress positive ideas upon your subconscious mind with hopeful feelings and then act on the idea. You have one life, there is no need to live it miserably. No one can make your day, months, or years great, but you. No one is in control, or responsible for making you happy. Others may contribute to your happiness, but they are not responsible for your happiness. Living your best life is totally up to you. You must do the things that bring you happiness and fulfillment. For me, that thing was discovering my purpose and actually doing the thing that I love. Life is too short to be too afraid to be lived. Take that leap, make that call, let your hair down and stretch yourself. If you are not enjoying life, have self-introspection and begin to make changes wherever they are needed. As you begin stepping outside of your comfort zone remember, Zechariah 4:10 encourages us to not despise small beginnings. Make it a great day by doing what makes you happy.

Own Your Choices

"Choices are fair, you always get what you choose."
Latrivette Williams

Our life is an accumulation of our choices. Whether we act in ignorance or in wisdom; we have acted. No human has ever been made to do anything against their will. No matter the weight of influence or the love for another, have we given up our freedom to choose for ourselves. The life we now live is a result of our choices. I am sure many people are on the edge of their seats waiting to tell someone about who is to blame for the condition of their life. As bad as we would like for it to be someone else's fault, it's not. We are in control of our thoughts, feelings, and actions. Whatever we project out into the universe whether positive or negative, it has ramifications. When we take ownership of our choices, we empower ourselves to no longer feel powerless to undesirable circumstances. As long as you place the blame on others for how your life has turned out, you will continue to get the same results because you don't see that it's your own thinking and choosing that has landed you where you are. You'll end up living the life you think you have to live instead of the one you truly desire because you don't believe that you have control of your life. Until you own up to your choices, you'll always expect more from others for your life than you expect from yourself. Blaming others puts you off the hook from having any part to play in your misfortune and totally places the blame on someone else demanding they fix your life so you can get on with it. If you are waiting for someone else to fix your life, don't hold your breath. No one can put your life on the right track but you. By deciding to take ownership, you are accepting things for what they are and are now able to deal with them and move past them.

Deuteronomy 30:19 says, "Today I have given you the choice between life and death, between blessings and curses. Now I call on heaven and earth to witness the choice you make. Oh, that you would choose life, so that you and your descendants might live!" Based upon Deuteronomy 30:19, God leaves the choices we make totally up to us, and He also informs us that those choices have consequences. The choices we make, determines the quality of life we live. Life mirrors back to us our most dominant feelings and beliefs. We are like magnets, attracting to ourselves the things we are in harmony with. Heaven and earth bear witness of the choices we make, God is not to blame, we are orchestrating the details of our own lives. His desire is that we will choose life-blessings, but he cannot fulfill that desire for us, the choice is ours to make. Whatever you bind on earth will be bound in heaven, and whatever you loose on earth will be loosed in heaven (see Matt. 18:18). This explains how Man can both receive both good and bad. Although God is sovereign, he doesn't control all things fully, yet. He is most definitely not causing bad things to happen to anyone. We have a mind of our own that follows whatever path we set it upon. As bad as we may not want to own up to the experiences we've had, we were the ones that attracted them into our lives. The universe being subjective and impressionable, mirrors back to us the ideas we impress upon it and present to us circumstances and situations that harmonize. We operate out of cause and effect; nothing ever just happens. Root and reason results in fruits and seasons. When I first found out about this, I recalled some things that I had experienced and wondered did I truly attract those experiences into my life. Truth is, I did. For whatever reasons, I attracted situations and circumstances into my life no matter how good or bad through the universal law of attraction. Knowing that our choices shapes our world, we can choose the best possible future for our lives. Our choices gives us the ability to take control of our lives and to express who we are and not who others want us to be. Because of choice, we have the opportunity to express free will. Because we have a choice, we can separate ourselves from things that are toxic and engage in things that give us life. We can create a new norm for our lives. Because we are not automatons, we are always thinking and choosing the details of our lives into existence. Up until now, you probably thought that life just happened, you probably thought you didn't have a say so in the matter, but you do. Own your choices and become empowered to change your life.

Should I Follow My Heart?

"The great thing about having a choice is, you can decide to be brave." Latrivette Williams

Should I follow my heart or should I suffer in fear? Do I reach beyond my present circumstances and move forward, or do I remain where I am because I know what I have, but not what I'm going to get? Most people have worn out their dancing shoes because they have danced around the idea of how they really envision their lives for far too long. They battle with what move they need to make. Even more, they are afraid of what they could lose if they make a move. They have one foot in and one foot out. They aren't smiling their best smile, laughing their hardest laugh, or living their best life. They are behind on their dreams and possibly short on money. I can relate. I remember having this great desire for a mentor. I believed a mentor would be a major factor in helping me bridge the gap from where I was, to where I wanted to be. This idea of having a mentor was suppressed upon my subconscious mind and my subconscious mind went to work to bring about my desire. Fast forward a bit, I got a mentor/life coach and my life haven't been the same. As a result, I made the decision to face my fears of writing and to move into the space of being a life coach. Having someone to help me put the pieces of my life together, helped transform my life into one that I'm proud and very fund of. I stretched myself beyond my old mental conditioning. I had not only decided to follow my heart, I did follow my heart. Because I stretched myself, I could no longer fit into the mold I was once accustomed to. I had outgrown the mold by transforming my paradigm. Following my heart wasn't suicide, to be honest when I was suppressing my desires, that's when I felt like a fish out of water. This new path was giving me life. If I'd stayed comfortable, conforming and reacting from my old paradigm, I wouldn't have begun to see the best version of myself. I believe one of the greatest gifts one can give to self, is the permission to be yourself.

John 10:10 B says, "I came that they may have and enjoy life, and have it in abundance." It took me a few years, but I realized that God has given me life to enjoy, visions to be explored, hope for the future and faith to endure. He has perfected everything that concerns us, I just had to live in that truth. When the Bible said our ways are not God's ways and our thoughts are not His thoughts, it never said that it had to stay that way, but it does explain the mental conditioning and state that man can reside in. There were times when I would read about being an overcomer because Christ has already overcame, but I would still have a defeated mindset. My thoughts were certainly not aligned with his wisdom and inevitably my ways contradicted beautiful truths God spoke about me. I was only offering lip service to God because my heart was so full of doubt and fear. This would also explain the knocking knees and timidity I felt once I actually decided to take a leap of faith. Once I began being true to my convictions of who I am, seeing my life as God sees it—without limitations and endless possibilities, it was a new normal I could get used to. There was indeed a war going on within me, my old paradigm fighting to remain, but I was and am, set on renewing my mind to living the life I love and loving the life I live. Don't allow fear to stop you from taking risks. Your whole life will be about taking risks. You'll never see how it'll all work out if you don't ever try it. There will always be some reason why you shouldn't do something. Take on the Nike attitude and just do it. I wasn't accustomed to this way of living or thinking but I braced myself as well as embraced this newness of life and adapted to a new norm. I changed things up a bit; instead of snoozing on life, I set goals that caused me to jump out of bed. Instead of finding reasons why I couldn't, I found reasons why I could. I stopped making excuses and started making opportunities for myself. I was excited about my future. No more one day or some day planning. I now write the vision plainly and follow wherever it leads me. By taking a step of faith every day, I am learning to walk with confidence. I am learning how to follow my heart. What is it that you've been holding back on? How many times have you ignored that tug for something more? I'm here to tell you that it will not go away. Unless you direct that energy in the direction of its intention, through the use of your imagination, will power, perception, reasoning, memory, and intuition- you'll live with the fact of only knowing that you were called to something greater. God put it this way, faith without works is dead (see James 2:17).

Choosing faith over fear is the objective. Your playing small by hiding behind fears, traditions, other people opinions, and the worlds standards only give reason for limits, limits you place on yourself when you buy into them. Once I realized this truth, I gave myself permission to be bold, my kind of beautiful, fulfilled, successful, and in control of my life. I stepped from under the shadow of my comfort zone and I interrupted my regular scheduled mental programming. I began making good on my plans concerning my future, a future a few years ago you couldn't have told me I had. I honestly thought my future was about me getting a job and eventually retiring. I had no idea that I had a passion for life coaching or let alone writing.

Acting on the intuition to ask for help in moving my life forward, was one of the best decisions I've made. It changed my life. We are all born for a purpose. We have a calling to fulfill. We have skills and talents to offer the world. No one else can be you and you can't be someone else, which is why it is imperative that you live out your true potential. The world called for you and you came, don't chicken out now. Life is about love and expression, express the God within you. Maybe you don't know the proper first move, start where you can and remember it's a process. Once you get started you'll attract into your life everything you need. I hope you decide to take a leap of faith with, or without all the details. With, or without support. Use every possible resource and reach for higher heights and deeper

PUSH

depths. Regardless of the motion in the ocean, stay the course and see your vision come to life. Most importantly, believe in you; know that you are equipped for the purpose and know that all good things pays off. Don't play it safe, live out your dreams.

Chapter 2

Who Are You Waiting On?

*"Everyone will not believe in you,
despite the lack of support
do it anyway."*
Latrivette Williams

If someone loses faith in your dream, it's okay. Your dream is your dream and it's on you to bring it into fruition, not them. Everyone you know might not enter into your promised land with you. Some will observe from afar and gossip, and some who we know as naysayers will tell you how it would never be possible, but those that believe in you will push you forward by whatever means they can. This reminds me of Caleb and Joshua and the people of Israel having to decide whose report they were going to believe. God had chosen the land of Canaan to be the place the Israelites would settle. Moses sent out Joshua, Caleb and ten other leaders to spy the land. They all returned and reported to Moses and the people what they observed. Their reports were divided, it was two against ten. Ten of the spies couldn't see the land as a place to settle. They saw themselves being too small to go up against the present inhabitants, actually they used the word "grasshoppers" (see Numbers 13:33). They could not see themselves taking the land that God had already told them was theirs. Because they saw themselves as being too weak, their report was negative and self-defeating. When the people heard this negative report they began to respond in fear by speaking negatively in-spite of the promise. Out of the twelve spies, Caleb and Joshua were the only two who came back with a good report in response to the promise. They saw what God had spoken about the land was true and they believed, with God they were able to overtake it. Because of the unbelief in the peoples heart as well as the ten spies, they were not able to enter the promised land. Those who responded in disbelief all died outside of the promise, in the wilderness wandering. However, Joshua and Caleb continued to look forward to that day, they outlived those of their generation and entered the promise land with the next generation that believed. The Israelites advanced upon the land and defeated the inhabitants and dwelled therein. Caleb and Joshua didn't enter with those they started out with. They didn't share the same vision so they couldn't share the same reality. When you believe all things are possible, no one, or thing can stop it from happening. Everyone will not believe in you or your dream and again that's okay. Don't allow this to discourage your heart, keep at it and do it anyway. If you have to stand alone, be willing to do just that.

Sometimes the people you think are ready to go with you, aren't. While pursuing your dreams, it's important to not keep company with those that are miserable. Nothing hurts more than when you are super excited about something and then you share it and the person you share it with response is very dry and critical. If you haven't developed a strong self-image, their criticism or dryness can penetrate your heart, choke your joy and rage war against your dreams. Don't wait on others to feel it or envision it, what you do with it is what matters, your dream impacts you more than anyone else. Treat your dream like you would treat a seed planted in the ground. Your dream is your seed. Your mind is the soil. The Word is the water that helps it grow. Guard your seed with all diligence. Nurture your soil so that it will remain rich. Tend to it daily to keep out the weeds of doubt. Though the vision that has been planted in your subconscious mind tarry, wait, it will definitely come to pass. During the process remember that your seed is alive, it's not dead. Although you may not see an instant manifestation, that doesn't mean that things aren't manifesting. Your seed (dreams) is moving from one form to the next. Once an actual seed is planted, it goes through the process of germination, this process happens underneath the soil away from our view. Because we know this little fact, we don't go digging up the seed every day to see if it is growing, we know that it's growing. Our dreams are like those seeds. In order to see our dreams manifest, it must go through a process. Just like the seed that's planted in the ground, we do not see every detail of its growth, but it's essential not to cancel out the life of the seed because you cannot track every moment of progress. The image you hold through your imagination is your evidence of life, it's the evidence of things not seen. Digging up a natural seed every day would be equivalent to operating in doubt and fear which can cause your soil (heart/mind) to become hard and unfruitful. There is a process to everything. Be patient and go through the process. Keep toiling the ground of your heart, then you'll see your harvest manifest into full bloom.

You don't need the validation of others to fulfill your calling. You owe it to yourself to live out your full potential. God is true to his nature even if every person is proved to be a liar. Be true to who you are, even if others around you aren't. As you set out into new territory, the right people at the right time in the right place will show up to walk with you. God made you for a reason, for a special purpose.

Don't waste time pondering on other people's opinion about you or your future unless they are using their influence for good. If I were you, that thing that you have been secretly desiring to do, but too afraid to do, I would get started on that very thing. It's what makes you you. If you don't fight for your dream, no one else will. No one else will be more passionate about your purpose than you. Dreams don't come true without perseverance and determination. Let the world know you are present and regardless of the amount of support you have or regardless of your circumstances, make your mark.

You Think You Have Forever

*"What are you waiting for?
You'll never fully enjoy your life,
until you neglect your comfort zone."
Latrivette Williams*

The Bible records three in a half-years of Jesus ministry. Jesus, according to scripture, was thirty-three years old when he was crucified. Although much of Jesus life is not mentioned and many stories are not written, we are made aware through scripture that He did mighty works, so much so that all could not be contained within the Bible. He accomplished so much within that short amount of time, that the stories are still being told. Jesus in the flesh knew he didn't have forever to live out his earthly purpose. He didn't sit around and hold his hands with Peter and the other eleven disciples, complaining about his circumstances or oppositions. Jesus knew the importance of time and had no problem with making the best of it. He was aware of it being a time for everything. He knew just as sure as he was born, there was going to be a time he would also have to die. It was apparent that he was on a mission and he knew he didn't have forever. He constantly pointed his disciples to his time of death. Although he prepared them for the inevitable, he also showed them how to make perfect use of their time, talent, and treasure. Timing was and is important to Jesus. In the book of Ecclesiastes, twenty-eight different situations was mentioned as being times and seasons of our lives. If Jesus being completely God in the flesh, was time conscious, that's a big indication that we should be also.

As kids, we are asked what we want to be when we grow up. I remember I wanted to become a teacher. Time moved on and my excitement for wanting to teach grade school dissipated. Two thousand four, I graduated without a clue as to what I wanted to do with my life. Between the time I was asked that question up until graduation, I'm sure that question got buried under other concerns and hobbies. As a child you have your parents or guardians taking care of you and all of your expenses so you're not worried about providing for yourself. What I wanted to be just didn't seem that important throughout the years. Looking back, I can remember a few months before graduating just deciding to find work, and I did, at a local grocery store making only minimum wage. I worked there for some time, still having no notion as to what my passion is. In fact, I worked several other jobs before I found my niche. Maybe you are like I was, stumbling over your own feet. The Bible says, "where there is no vision the people perish (see Proverbs 29:18). My life was a mess and there were no excuses. I can't go back in time and change things, but by having a vision for my life now, I can sense what the rest of my life will be like. How does a man or woman change their ways or their path? By the renewing of the mind through the perfect wisdom and word of God. That's why when a person changes their ways, they don't look like what they've been through. Their past says they are supposed to be broke, busted and disgusted, but they altered their future by changing their paradigm. They didn't go back in time into their past, they began with the time they had before them and they changed the trajectory of their future. As long as breath is in your body you have time to change your life and redirect your path.

Because time is so precious, you want to make every day count for something great. Do what ignites the happiness within you today. Don't wait for all conditions to be favorable, all conditions may never be favorable, but step out anyway. Every time we make excuses for why we aren't acting on God given ability, we lie to ourselves about why we aren't operating in our greatness.

Ecclesiastes 11:4 says, "Farmers who wait for perfect weather never plant. If they watch every cloud, they never harvest." The timing may never be just right, but he that observes only, never plant to receive a harvest. No one will invest more in you than you. Don't listen to the naysayers that tell you: you've waited too late, you're too old, you're not smart enough, capable, or ready. Sure, living outside of your comfort zone can be frightening, you'll be vulnerable, and afraid, but I encourage you to put one foot before the other and make one commitment at a time. Don't wait any longer, live your best life.

God Cares!

"Give all your worries and cares to God, for he cares about you." 1 Peter 5:7

Some people think that God is so busy that he does not have the time to care for them. 1 Peter 5:7 informs us that we can give our cares to God because of the simple fact that he does care about us. Hebrews 4:16 says, "So let us come boldly to the throne of our gracious God. There we will receive his mercy, and we will find grace to help us when we need it most." Worry often rises when we believe the idea that our problems or situations cannot or may not be resolved. Although we verbally speak that all things are working for our good, we become impatient, feeling as though God has abandoned us in our distress. We pray but after we have prayed our faith last only a short moment because we don't see change immediately. We desperately want relief, we panic and become fearful. During our time of being afraid we retract from our initial response which was casting our cares upon God and trusting his guidance. Because our faith was short lived, we took matters into our own hands. We created bills, wrecked friendships, acted violently and made other reckless decisions in an attempt to fix our problem. We acted independently of God, all because we believed that God didn't care. More and more people are confused with who God is and the roll that he play in their lives and for good reasons. God get blamed for a lot, but the question that is not being asked by many is, are the accusations true? When tragedies occur, we are told not to question God because his will must be done. But, is God the one to blame or are we responsible for the tragedies we see? 1 John 1:5 says, "This then is the message which we have heard of him, and declare unto you, that God is light, and in him is no darkness at all." God cannot be the one that's causing darkness to come about in our lives because there is no darkness in him. When someone is in poverty, it's often asked, "what will it profit a man to gain the whole world and lose his soul (see Matthew 16:26)?" Some how this scripture has been taught in a way that gives the impression that wealth will lure you away from God, that abundance is bad, but 2 Corinthians 8:9 states, "For you know the grace of our Lord Jesus Christ, that, though he was rich, yet for your sake he became poor, so that you through his poverty might become rich." God doesn't desire to have those he love, lack the things they need, but he also knew and stated in scripture that the poor would be among us always (see Mark 14:7). God knew despite his provision that some would still live in poverty because of their unbelief in his provision of abundance. When a loved one has passed away, we are told, God has need of them and that he has called them home. John 10:10B states "I have come that they may have life, and have it to the full." God gives life, not take it. Unfortunately people, especially those of the faith, have a hard time casting their cares upon a benevolent God because they have a hard time seeing him as benevolent. All they see is him taking from them and causing them grief. The picture of a loving God has been changed to a picture of a God who punishes to show his love or who take in order to give something to you. His character has taken hit after hit. No wonder we have a hard time trusting him, we don't know if he is very trusting. Because of this, many people have fallen away and many are reluctant to come into the faith. Ask yourself, would he really go through the trouble of creating all of creation for us, if he didn't care for us? He made us after his likeness, he wants nothing more than to have a relationship with us, and provide our every need. But it's no strange thing why it's 2019 and we still need to have this discussion. The question of, "Is God good?" has been going on for a long time now. We aren't the only generation that struggled with knowing the character of God, the Israelites struggled to believe that God was and is good also, they asked Moses, did God deliver us from the hand of Pharaoh to kill us? The answer was no, again there is no darkness in him. God loved them with undying love. God delivered them from the bondage of Pharaoh, made a vow to be their God, promised them land to dwell in, with the intentions of giving them a better life. They needed food, he fed them. They were thirsty, he gave them water. They needed a leader he gave them Moses. We needed a savior, He gave himself. God didn't deliver us from the hands of Satan, to in turn treat us harshly and desert us. Romans 8:38-39 reads, "And I am convinced that nothing can ever separate us from God's love. Neither death nor life, neither angels nor demons, neither our fears for today nor our worries about tomorrow-not even the powers of hell can separate us from God's love. No power in the sky above or in the earth below- indeed, nothing in all creation will ever be able to separate us from the love of God that is revealed in Christ Jesus our Lord." Everything that God does is centered around love. Because of the misunderstanding of the character of God, people are lacking confidence in his compassion towards them. They are not easily swayed by his loving call to confidently cast their cares upon him. Today, hear his call to care for you and harden not your heart. Hear his call today, trust him. Trust him because he loves you best. Trust him because he is wisdom and he wants to direct your path. He will never leave you, so you never have to worry about facing life alone. Keep in mind that God created laws to govern the universe, laws that we must live by. The choice to operate with these laws is up to us. When we violate or comply with these laws, we in return reap the fruit of our choices. The condition of our choices determines the condition of our results. God's universal laws are flawless, we on the other hand don't always comply flawlessly with these laws. Through Jesus, hope was given to a corrupt world order, he died for us in our place that we might believe in him and confess him as our Lord and Savior. As children of God we take our place of right standing with God because of Jesus. As Sons and Daughters we are to embrace and explore our relationship with him and allow his Kingdom agenda to become our agenda. His modus operandi should be our modus operandi that his Kingdom come on earth as it is in heaven through us. As it has been declared by Jesus, the Kingdom of God is within us (see Luke 17:20-21). As a born-again believer we reign in Christ, the choices we make matters, they affect everything. The laws of God are not partial. They affect you whether you know them or not. He gives us scripture for our learning and application. He says, I am the way and the truth and the life (see John 14:6). Even if you don't quite understand what's going on in your life, know that you can trust that He's good and that He's for you.

Jeremiah 29:11 (NIV) says, "For I know the plans I have for you," declares the Lord, "plans to prosper you and not to harm you, plans to give you hope and a future."

Psalm 115:11 says, "All you who fear the Lord, trust the Lord! He is your helper and your shield." Be affirmed in the fact that God is a shield and helper to those that reverence him. Isaiah 59:1 says, "Listen, The Lord's arm is not too weak to save you, nor is his ear too deaf to hear you call." If you have ever doubted if God has heard you, know that he's not deaf and that he hears your call and he's able to see you through any situation.

God sacrificed his only son for all humanity. There is absolutely no depth he's not willing to go, to show his love for us. He has never given us reason to believe he can't be trusted. He has shown us the love and compassion he has toward us.

"Let not your heart be troubled. You believe in God; believe also in me" (John 14:1). Through the highs and lows, put your trust in God and remember that he cares about you and everything that concerns you. He is very fund of you, you have always been the apple of his eyes.

Be Mindful With Whom You Share

*"Be selective with whom you share your problems,
because only few people care others are just curious."*
Sushan Sharma

It is human nature to be social and to share our lives with others. The things we share can range from very small matters like our favorite color or big matters like finances or dreams concerning our future. When we feel as though we can trust someone, there are no boundaries as to the things we share. Unfortunately, some have been found unworthy of knowing the intimate and very important details of our lives. When there has been a breach of trust, someone has betrayed or disappointed us, we become reluctant to risk so much again. We learn in a very painful way that we should be mindful with whom we share precious pieces of our lives with. I love quotes and the one above rings true. Some people who ask about your well-being are just curious, not concerned. Some people just want to know if you're doing better than they are. Sometimes they call you just to find out if your Facebook status true; are you faking it until you make it, or are things really going that good for you. You can sense they don't have your best interest at heart by the tone of their voice and the cheap shots they take at your self-esteem. Don't take it personal, the issue is not really with you, it's with them. Instead of them effectively communicating their truth whatever that may be, they became critical and negative. They allowed negativity to come into their hearts, the one thing we are called to watch with all diligence. Proverbs 4:23 says, "Guard your heart above all else, for it determines the course of your life." Our hearts determines what path we take in life, it is also easily influenced which is why we must be mindful with whom we share it with. Once we share our hearts, we are subjecting ourselves to other people opinions about our circumstances as well as who they think we are. There is this old adage I remember saying when I was a little girl that says, "sticks and stones may break my bones but words will never hurt me." Boy was I wrong, words can hurt. Based upon where we are emotionally, mentally, and spiritually the wrong words said at the wrong time can cause an immense impact on our self-esteem. We are especially vulnerable to other people opinions about our lives when we have a weak self-image and are in a vulnerable state. Telling the wrong person the intimate delicacies of our heart can be dis-empowering. If you are unsure as to who you can trust with certain matters, ask Holy Spirit to lead you to the right person. Who we tell matters. Good counsel soothes and moves the soul, but bad counsel can wound the soul. When we share with others, depending upon the state of mind that person is in, their advice could be like water that nourishes a seed, or it could be like thorns that grow up with the seed and choke it. Cultivate the garden of your heart, guard it with all diligence. Surround yourself with those that celebrate you and those that genuinely celebrate with you. Loyalty isn't worth a hill of beans if it is not bringing life and growth to your soul.

Chapter 3

When Things Get Hard, You Mustn't Quit

"Who knows the joy of finishing, except the one who finishes"
Latrivette Williams

I know there isn't a person in the world that haven't experienced some form of a challenge. At some point of your life you may have felt like everything was going haywire. Once you got one thing in order, two other challenges took place. Some would say, "If it isn't one thing, it's another." You may have thought if one more thing goes wrong, I'm going to lose it. You've taken all that you can take. During those very challenging, yet pivotal moments, it is very vital that you become encouraged and dare yourself not to give up. Jesus knew that we all would experience difficulty. He knew what impact they would have on us, so, he inspired John to write us a very heart-warming verse of scripture, letting us know what He has done for us. If read in faith, it has the power to quite our raging inner turmoil. John 16:33 says, "These things I have spoken to you, so that in Me you may have peace. In the world you have tribulation, but take courage; I have overcome the world." God has fought the fight and now it's fixed for you. Your position now regarding anything is the position of victory, whether it feel like it or not. In most cases when we feel defeated by our circumstances, it's because we've told ourselves some wacky story of how it'll never work out. Having said that, we've reached a place where we lack fortitude. Spiritually we are weak because we aren't sure of our rights and privileges and physically we've worn ourselves out with all the negative thinking we've done. Quitting seems like the only way to cope with the circumstances and situations. It is at this point we've made our mole hill a mountain and no longer feel in control of the situation. Dangerous levels of stress; fear, and worry have set our gear in motion to give up. "What's the use anyway?" becomes our attitude. More often than we want to admit, in the mist of adversity we've forgotten our God given truth and panicked. We habitually imagine the worst possible outcome. In those moments when we are faint of heart, it's not because our circumstances have the advantage, it's because we can't seem to see past them. God has predestined us to live a victorious life, but many people scratch their heads in dismay because of the lack of victories they have experienced.

It is important to know that anything you imagine is real, whether good or bad. If you believe defeat, you'll receive defeat. If you believe victory, you'll receive victory. It shall be to you according to your faith. I remember the story about David when he fought Goliath. Goliath would taunt the Israelites army daily, no one would dare accept his challenge to fight because they were all afraid. David was the youngest of his brothers. He looked after the sheep and the goats, while his brothers were soldiers in King Saul's army. One day, David's dad called for David to check on his brothers and to give them food. While checking on his brothers, Goliath the nine to ten feet giant came out and challenged anyone who was brave enough to fight him. They would have to fight until one was defeated by death. David started asking around about the reward for killing Goliath, King Saul got wind of his curiosity and summoned David into his presence. King Saul didn't think David was the right person for the job, but because David insisted, King Saul gave him permission to advance. With a brave heart, David was ready to take Goliath down. David didn't see his victory against Goliath as an impossible outcome, instead he saw all things being possible with God. David remembered there had been other challenges in his life. When lions and bears tried to eat up the lamb, David would kill them with a club. David believed that God was with him. David ran toward the opposition rather than relenting in fear and killed Goliath the giant. Had he not had the courage to face Goliath, the Israelites would have continued to be taunted and trapped by their circumstances. Many people are startled in their tracks because of the opposition they face. They are challenged to become brave; to stand up against internal and external fears. We mustn't become trapped in our challenges, we should use them as a catalyst to help us grow into a greater awareness of what we are capable of. Again, John 16:33 says, "I have told you all this so that you may have peace in me. Here on earth you will have many trials and sorrows. But take heart, because I have overcome the world." As you look over your life, don't focus on the problems, keep your attention on God and the life he has called you to. If you focus on the negatives, you'll develop the negatives. When your thoughts aren't flowing in harmony with things that are praise worthy, of a good report, true, right, noble, pure, or lovely; it can distract you from what's good in your life (see Philippians 4:8).

    If you give up, you will not see your plans unfold. If you quit, you accept defeat. Keep moving forward. Persistence is key.

The Word of God is Practical

"And the Word was made flesh, and dwelt among us"
John 1:14

From Genesis to Revelation, God demonstrates the practicality of his Word. Through the life of Jesus, the principles of God were demonstrated for our usage and for the purpose of developing a faith-based relationship with God. Through his examples and instructions and through his grace and mercy towards us, we can trust his principles for our lives. He calls us to live by the same standards that he lived by. He called the world into existence by speaking things that were not as though they were, he calls us to do the same. He healed the sick and he raised the dead, he calls us to do the same. He prayed, he calls us to pray. He didn't borrow from anyone, we are called to owe no man nothing. He gave to the poor, he calls us to give to the poor as well. He respected those that were around him. He loved, even when it didn't seem so easy to do. He forgave men of their sins. He wept with those that mourned and he rejoiced with those who rejoiced. Jesus showed us what it's like to live a principle driven, God loving, happy, fulfilling life. He showed us that God's principles are not heavy (burdensome), indeed they are light and they should be the yoke that guides our lives. The Word is practical; designed for actual use. In every book of the Bible, principles are at work. God suggest and informs us of universal principles because his will is that we will not live in ignorance. God informs us of these things that we might get the most out of our human experience. For this reason, in whatever situation or circumstance we are in, we can live and speak the word of God and it'll work for our good. If the Word wasn't practical, God who is ever merciful and abundantly gracious would have never expected us to govern our lives by it. The examples of the Bible are for our learning and practical usage. God became flesh and blood and lived among us. Jesus gave reference and reverence to the Word. When he was tempted by the Devil, Jesus knew just how to respond. He gleaned from scriptures that were befitting to his situation and he spoke them as a defense against the temptation. Jesus leaned on the principles of God to keep him grounded. Jesus in the flesh lived by every principle. His objective wasn't to show off about who he is, but to show us how much alike him we are and what we can do when we apply the Word to our character, situation and circumstance. "But be doers of the word, and not hearers only, deceiving yourselves (James 1:22)." Speak the word, visualize the word working for you, and allow the word to move you into corresponding action.

Biblical Principles Work

"Do not let this Book of the Law depart from your mouth; meditate on it day and night, so that you may be careful to do everything written in it. Then you will be prosperous and successful." Joshua 1:8, NIV

How many of us purchase equipment that need to be assembled and we throw the instructions away? Many of us do, I know I have. After you've spent some time on the project, after having thrown away the instructions, frustration and anger tends to set in. What would have taken you an hour with the instructions have now taken three hours, and the main reason why you threw away the instructions was to save some time and prove that you are smart enough to get the job done on your own. When you started the project you were confident that you knew enough to assemble the equipment without any input from the manufacturer. But after a few hours of not getting the results you desire, you realize how important and necessary it is to follow the manufacturer's instructions. When we ditch out on the instructions we find out the hard way that the creator of the product knows best. When we make attempts to assemble, or operate something without following the instructions, sometimes the product isn't stable, it wobbles, sometimes it's left to be finished one day or it doesn't function as properly it should. How many times have our lives been treated like a piece of furniture? Instead of following the principles of life, we set them aside and make up rules as we go. When we ditch instructions and fail to adhere the principles of the Word, we are saying, I know a way, it may not be the way, but I still believe it'll get me the same results. But the truth is it never does. Proverbs 14:12 says, "There is a way that seems right to a man, but in the end it leads to death." There is our way then there is God's way. Our way, is unstable, questionable and very frustrating. Doing things our way often leads us to dark places in our lives. Places of guilt, shame, doubt, fear and other low energy emotions. If you have been living your life like you've been assembling your furniture, and you're unhappy with the results you've been getting, check your values. Your values are connected to the principles you keep and the beliefs you hold. Your values are motivating your actions and if the actions you are seeing aren't lining up with God's principles, adjust your values.

The scriptures tell us to meditate on the word of God day and night, that we may make our way successful. If we pattern our lives after the principles of God, we will inevitably make our way successful (scripture referenced above). The word of God need to be before our eyes, in our ears, and in our hearts every day on every occasion that our hearts may be guided in the right direction (see Proverbs 4:20–21). I've tried doing things apart from the wisdom of God and was hard pressed. Things just didn't work out the way they should have. When I was supposed to love, I disliked. When I was supposed to forgive, I held on to anger. When I should have gone this way, I went that way. And although I speak on this matter, I'm not perfect in always carrying out this principle. I still find myself at times doing the thing that I should not do. But I've worked against the principles enough to know that it's better to just obey. God's principles are set in place to help us experience a happy, fulfilling, long, and satisfying life. In the event when we go against his wisdom, we open our lives up to opposition. Like Adam and Eve, because we don't see death immediately when we violate the principles of God, we continue to eat from what is forbidden.

Take the principle of finances for instance, Paul instructs us by the influence of Holy Spirit not to owe anyone anything except to love them (see Romans 13:8), but some of us including myself have experienced going out and financing things that we didn't have the money to purchase. We've grown accustom to borrowing money, even at the expense of an interest rate. Everything from necessity to pleasure is placed on credit. While we're borrowing, we don't see immediate repercussions so we keep on biting until we're faced with more month than money. In a moment of desperation for relief, we realize that the ways of God are life and they do make our ways successful, if we follow them. When we violate the laws of God we feel the pain of violating, we don't see progression as we should. When we work in harmony with the laws, we see movement in the right direction.

Principles are set in place for a reason, they keep everything flowing in a decent, fair and orderly manner. Biblical principles work if we work them. Whether we fail to work with, or are ignorant of them, God will not suspend his universal laws for anyone, to do so he would have to show favoritism and God is no respecter of persons (see Romans 2:11). Work the word, because it will work for you.

This Too Shall Pass

*"For our momentary, light distress (this passing trouble)
is producing for us an eternal weight of glory (a fullness)
beyond all measure (surpassing all comparisons, a transcendent splendor
and an endless blessedness)!"*
2 Corinthians 4:17, AMP

The law of polarity states that everything has an opposite. If you have an up, you also have a down, an in and an out, uproar and peace, night and day, summer and winter. To say it another way, whatever we are experiencing, the opposite is equally present. Its what side of the coin we choose to focus on that matters. The trouble we are having is understanding that trouble don't last always. Some people hit a hard spot in life and give up. They stop putting forth any effort to see positive change in their lives. They sometimes hold an, "it is what it is" type attitude. They have given in to the darkness of hopelessness. Because they are so focused on the negative, they can't see the positive. They are embedding themselves in negativity, yet they wonder will their storm ever pass. They develop learned helplessness, they feel as though they can't catch a break, they are always complaining about life dealing them a bad hand. They become immobilized by distress. There are moments in our lives, when our inner two-year-old self is triggered; we want to throw tantrums, scream, kick, and point our fingers at those who we think are to blame. When we are going through unpleasant situations, we quickly forget biblical wisdom as well as who we are in Christ, and we begin to see ourselves as hopeless. We become less aware of our ability to soar and to overcome. Our unpleasant situation or circumstance isn't forever, it's only temporary and if we allow it to, it has the power to transform us.

We must remember Christ in us, the hope of glory (see Colossians 1:27). Rather than developing a learned helplessness, we must adapt the attitude of a victor. Instead of only seeing trouble and misery, we must be open to seeing the lesson and the blessing amid such difficult circumstances. When trouble arises and it will arise, we shouldn't become fixated on the trouble. When we become fixated on the problem, we create an even bigger problem and instead of giving energy to a solution, we are giving more energy to our problem.

1 Corinthians 10:13 (Mirror Bible) says, "Your situation is not unique! Every human life faces contradictions! Here is the good news: God believes in your freedom! He has made it possible for you to triumph in every situation that you will ever encounter!" When we are heavily burdened we are at times embarrassed and feel as though we are the only ones who have experienced, or is experiencing what we are facing. The agony of pain and heaviness of shame, leaves one feeling that there is no way of escape. Know that there are others, others who have faced the same circumstances and have found their freedom. Their storm came and passed away. We know from scripture that our afflictions are not meant to last forever. We are to learn from them and move on from them. For, life consists of growth and liberation. The reason being that some storms last so long is not because God is dragging them out, but because we aren't growing through them.

If we're not growing through them, then we are creating cycles. Some things take us years to understand and grow through and some don't. As it happens, our mindset can be so negative towards our circumstances that even if we have positive thoughts, they are few and far between and even then, we consciously reject it because of the negative image we've believed and reinforced time and time again. The memories of past experiences seem to haunt us and the only mental pictures we can phantom for our future are the ones we least desire. This type of mindset has many people: lonely, skeptical, depressed, stagnant, and even fearful. Time moved on, but they didn't. Frustration and pain are as fresh as the day it happened. It has immobilized them and dictated their lives. However, there is consolation available. We aren't stuck because we have to be, we are stuck because we allow ourselves to be. There is always a way of escape. God is present, in that place where you became mentally, spiritually, emotionally, physically stuck. He's urging you to love, heal, forgive, grow, and move forward. Don't allow momentary displeasure to become a lifetime of pain. Situations and circumstances, come to pass.

2 Corinthians 4:8–9 (NIV) states, "We are hard pressed on every side, but not crushed; perplexed, but not in despair; persecuted, but not abandoned; struck down, but not destroyed." You are able to get up and brush yourself off after every challenge because you are impregnable. You haven't been able to look forward because you've been spending most of your time looking back. Re-evaluate the situation and see if there is some degree of good in it that you can hold on to, I bet it's something you over looked no matter how bad the situation is. Don't quit when you face something that appear to be more than you can handle, because there is nothing you can't handle. You are mighty through God. There is a time for everything, decide today, this too shall pass.

Chapter 4

Love: The Essence of Life

"Whoever does not love does not know God.
Because God is love. (1 John 4:8)

The world and its inhabitants have its origin in love. 1 John 4:8 tells us that God, our heavenly Father and creator, is love. Love is the greatest force there is. Love breaks barriers, makes a house a home, inspires heroism, sacrifices, and feed those that are hungry. Love is compassionate, forgiving, optimistic, selfless, and sees good in all people. Love is free, creative, and comforting. It does not seek to judge or hold grudges, but love seeks to understand. Love moves us into action. When we release love, we release light into the world. Love brings out the best in us. Love is energizing and eternal. It urges us to do more, know more, and not give up. Love inspires hope. Love never fails. When we make the choice to emit love, we are making the choice to give of ourselves liberally and unconditionally. Love is the greatest command given to man by God. Love is what connects us all together. By love, miraculous and marvelous works takes place, faith works by love (see Galatians 5:6). When we love, evil has no place to express itself in our hearts. Proverbs 10:12 says, "Hatred stirs up strife, but love covers all sins." Love brings out the best in all of us. However, we don't always operate in flow of this unconditional power. Sometimes we allow anger, hatred, and even jealousy to get the better of us. There may have been moments when you have struggled with loving someone, maybe that person wasn't so nice to you, they were difficult to deal with, critical and self-centered. And because you felt attacked, and disrespected you retaliated. As a result, you become madder than ever. The verdict of your heart is ready to deliberate and it has ruled in favor of disliking that person. Just like that and just that quick, we size people up. Poor communication, misunderstandings, and snappy judgements are recipes for disaster. People haven't talked to each other in years for one or more of these reasons. I've found out, the best way to get along with everyone, is to love them. And to be able to do this, I would have to look at the love of Jesus so that it can be my guide. The only way we know how to love, is because Christ first loved us. There is no better way to love others, except to love thyself with true mercy and grace.

Luke 6:31 says, "Do to others as you would have them do to you." It takes seeing ourselves in others, to lovingly do to others as we so desire to have them do to us. Let us keep in mind, how we respond to others isn't left up to them to decide. If someone isn't kind, respectful, caring, etc., that persons inconsistency with the law of love, doesn't give us a right away to retaliate. A gentle answer deflects anger, but a harsh word stirs up anger (see Proverbs 15:1). As you grow through life, know that every new level of your life will demand a different you. As we grow, we mature and with maturity comes new levels of how we should now be responding to things. We will not truly know how to treat others as we desire to be treated, until we learn how to love ourselves through the love that Christ has shown us. Truth be told, we can all be difficult at times, which is why instead of us flying off the handle at others, we can take a moment and find likeness in them and be patient with them. Galatians 6:1 says, "Brethren, if a man be overtaken in a fault, ye which are spiritual, restore such an one in the spirit of meekness; considering thyself, lest thou also be tempted." We are called to love our neighbor as ourselves (see Matthew 22:39, Mark 12:31). As we choose the principle of loving others as ourselves; we are choosing to forgive because we know what it's like to need forgiveness. We are choosing to respond in humility because we know that we are no greater than the next person. We are choosing to have joy over what is good in someone else life because we know what it feels like to experience bad. We are choosing to be patient. We are choosing to be kind. And we are choosing to see the good in everyone, because in spite of how much we mess up, we know that everything that God made was good. When we've reached a place where we feel that we do not like someone as I've mentioned earlier, we've forgotten to love them and instead we've treated them as though they were the Enemy. Instead of forgiving them or having patience with them, we've held their wrong against them and sentence them to no love. When we hold things against others we find it very difficult to find likeness in them. And when we can't find likeness in others, opposition is sure to rear its ugly head. When we fail to see ourselves in others, instead of trying to reconcile or understand them or the situation, we are quick to dismiss them and reject them. We should seek first to understand, rather than first demanding to be understood. Many people who appear to be difficult, are very guarded and hurt individuals. Not everyone walks around with their hearts on their sleeves. Don't take it personal when you encounter a person that seems to be too difficult to get along with. When we experience what is often the effects of the pain and hurt of what someone has once experienced or are still experiencing, we should take on an empathetic attitude in hopes of restoring that person. No man is meant to be an island. Like an onion, people have many layers, but to know them is to love them. When we express grace and mercy, we are more susceptible to seeing our neighbor as we see ourselves. All of us are worth making a big deal over. We are all worthy of compassion. We are all worth the time and the attention to be understood. When we drop our rocks of judgment and choose to understand each other better, we'll understand that everyone is worthy of love. John 13:35 says, "Your love for one another will prove to the world that you are my disciples." Love never fails! You may ask, what does love have to do with me following my dreams and manifesting my God-given potential? Holding grudges, being prideful, being very negative, and unfriendly is destructive to your health and to your success. We are also our best example of how we want to be treated. People may sometimes forget your name, what you're selling, and even the titles you hold, but they'll always remember how you caused their heart to feel.

The Principle of Sowing and Reaping

"Reaping comes with sowing" Latrivette Williams

We have all at some point in our lives sown a seed of promise into the chambers of our hearts; whether it was a promise made within relationships, or a promise from God. Immediately after hearing the promise, if not five seconds later thoughts, of doubt and fear comes like a thief to take the seed of promise away. In those very mind boggling moments, we learn what condition our hearts are in. Are we in a space to receive the promise that has been made to us? Are we willing to allow patience to perfect her work? Are we willing to endure persecution? Are we self-disciplined? Are we willing to see it through? Do we believe that it is possible? The condition of our hearts can be in various states: stony, shallow, gullible, rich and fertile. If our hearts are stony, we aren't receptive of the promise. We doubt its validity and unfortunately the promise can't take root. It as if we hear it but don't hear it. If our hearts are shallow, when doubt and fear present themselves, the seed will be easily uprooted because it lacks depth. If our hearts are gullible, we may see some sign of manifestation, but because we are easily deceived and easily distracted, what we have manifested will not mature. If our hearts are rich and fertile- full of unwavering faith and right believing, we cancel out the doubts and fears that come against the promise and eventually reap thirty, sixty, and even a hundred times more than what was sown (see Mark 4:14-20). Allow your potential to fill you with possibilities that will sprout and blossom into full maturity. The condition of our hearts (minds) determine the fruit we will bear. If we're not intentional with thinking in agreement

PUSH

with the promise, we'll end up thinking out of agreement and end up getting something we don't want. Don't exchange the promise for a lie. Whatever you sow, whether faith or fear, you will always reap what you sow.

Patience Perfect Work

"But let patience perfect its work, that you may be perfect and complete, lacking nothing." James 1:4

Patience is the virtue we least exercise when faced with ordeals. When the heat is on, we often feel anxious about getting the results we desire, instantaneously. Having patience in these intense and pressuring moments just doesn't seem to weigh in much. It's in James 1:4, where we are reminded that patience have a perfect work in our lives. Whenever we are face to face with contradictions, we can hold fast on the battle field of the mind by fighting the good fight of faith. As we stand our ground in faith, we will inevitably become unmovable. It is important to know as we delve deeper into the perfect work of patience, that our minds must agree, we must be of one mind. We often mess up when we pray one way, but speak and live another way. The Bible states that a double-minded man is unstable in all of his ways. It goes on to say that a double-minded man shouldn't expect to receive anything from the Lord (see James 1:6-8). What we speak and what we do, often contradict. After we have prayed, our mind, mouth and mannerisms should be in corresponding action with our prayer. But what happens a lot of the time is that we start off in faith, but because of the wait, we quickly move into fear. Have you ever said, or heard someone say, I don't have time to wait? Instead of allowing God to direct our steps, we lean to our own understanding which always lead to us doing something silly. We often forget in our moments of agony and our quest for immediate relief and results, that the thing that we have prayed about is already ours as an act of us naming and claiming it. If we would learn how to be in patience, which is to confidently endure by responding in faith to everyone, thing, and thought that comes up against the promise, patience will perfect its work, and we will no doubt possess and experience what we've already laid claims on. Although patience sounds like a small fish in a big pond, it is where many of us fall short because we don't understand how is it that we already have what we prayed for when we don't yet see it, taste it, smell it, touch it, or hear it. Faith is the link that holds our two worlds together. Faith is the substance of things hoped for, the evidence of the things not seen (see Hebrews 11:1). The spiritual realm is more real than what we see, since what we see has its origin in it. Faith affords us the advantage to see the "substance" in living color and in full form long before it's in our possession. By faith, Colonel Harland David Sanders saw "KFC" long before it manifested. Because of faith, he was persistent even in the most challenging moments, because he couldn't get away from the substance he had already seen. We are told that when we pray, believe, and receive what we ask for in faith. The moments between the spiritual prototype and manifestation requires time. Without engaging our six mental faculties upon our point of focus, we can easily become distracted and begin operating in unbelief. Our mental faculties work together both consciously and subconsciously to help bring our desires into manifestation. Our mental faculties are: will-power, intuition, imagination, memory, perception, and reasoning. By the usage of our six mental faculties given to us by God, we are guided to the places we need to go, the people we need to be around, the things we need to do and the things we need to put away. Although your present situation may contradict the image you hold, know that it must not contradict for long. What you hold in your mind, must transform what's without. With will-power and positive reasoning, remain focused on the ultimate goal and affirm that the image you hold is real. Recall as many helpful and encouraging memories as possible. Don't ignore your hunches, that's intuition knocking at your door with insight you weren't aware of. Perceive the best. Be aware of doubtful thoughts, once you allow yourself to believe in them, your life become like the billowing surge out at sea. One minute you're here and the next minute you're there. You're all over the place but accomplishing nothing. One day you believe and one day you don't. With every doubtful thought that penetrates your heart, your confidence becomes bleak. In order for us to receive the thing we hope for, we must be of one mind, not caught between two opinions. We must be definite upon the outcome we truly desire, regardless of the conditions. Stay the course and keep the faith, we are not always told the length of time in which we will see what we desire manifest, neither are we told every detail at once; however, we are called to walk by faith and to trust the principles of God in the process.

When a farmer goes out to farm, the most valuable thing the farmer have is the seeds in which he will plant. As he looks over the ground, he doesn't see anything but fertile soil. As he plants each seed in the ground he know that he will not get immediate results, yet he still choose to plant them anyway. He is not able to see every detail unfold as the seed grows and he's not really sure when exactly it will fully sprout, but he never goes out and dig up the seeds. He tends the ground and patiently expect a bumper crop harvest.

2 Corinthians 10:5 says, "Casting down imaginations and every high thing that exalts itself against the knowledge of God, bringing every thought into captivity to the obedience of Christ." Any thought that isn't in line with the truth of God is posing a threat to what you are believing God for. You must arrest it, hold it captive—reject it, don't allow it to contaminate your soil, I mean your beliefs.

Psalm 27:13 (KJV) states, "I had fainted, unless I had believed to see the goodness of the Lord in the land of the living." David said he would have despaired, but he believed to see God's goodness. Allow patience to have its perfect and pleasing work of perfection and completeness in your life. When things contradict the promise, know that God forewarned you that anything you ask in his name, is yours (see John 14:14). Allow patience to keep the seed of promise in the ground, so that you may reap your harvest.

The Peace of Praise

"Praise, a choice to be content in whatever state."
Latrivette Williams

Nothing manifests peace and encouragement like a thankful heart. You could be having the most challenging character building day, but it's something about checking out of the mental and emotional commotion and choosing to focus your attention on gratitude.

Have you ever been frantic about something and you just felt depleted? Depleted of joy, motivation, strength, will-power, and even faith? You just wanted to be left alone, unbothered, so you could soak in your misery. While it's so important to express how you feel rather than suppress the way you feel, it is also important to have peace about the situation or condition you are in. When we are flustered and agitated, everything seems off balance. When our hearts are heavy, we just want relief. One of the most natural effortless ways to lift our countenance is praise. Praise impacts us spirit, soul, and body. When we are in the act of praise, we are out of our heads and into our hearts. When we choose to praise God rather than complain, it has a way of liberating us. Giving thanks for all the good that we have in our lives is refreshing, it reassures us of who is for us, and just how fortunate and blessed we are. When we give praise, we are more capable of seeing things differently- more clearly. It is in the very act of praise that we have peace within and peace amid the situation; praise nurtures the soul. Have you ever praised anyone? It didn't matter if you knew them, or not. When you praised that person, you not only nurtured them, you nurtured your soul as well. That's because praise is twofold, it not only places the person you are praising in high regard, but you are also lifting yourself up as well. You feel good about saying something good about someone else. Adoration causes us to become joyful. This is the effect that praise can have on us which is important because, the most difficult part about being in a tough or unpleasant situation is the emotional feeling we feel. Praise have the ability to shift our emotional state. Even if your situation has not changed, because of the way you feel while expressing gratitude, your outlook of the situation can completely change. Gratitude is so effective at lifting your countenance because nothing says: rich, blessed, happy, or content like praise. When we are in a state of gratitude we exchange the feeling of lousiness for happiness. In a matter of minutes we can change our perception. Whenever the Israelites went up for battle in the Old Testament, praisers would go forth before the warriors. When praise went forth, the Israelites were reminded of the person they were giving praise to, and it also put them in remembrance of the battles they had won. When we praise God, it gives us renewed strength, boldness, confidence, and security.

When you lift Him up, you're inevitably building yourself up because you are made in his image and after his likeness (see Genesis 1:27).

Psalm 103:2 says, "Bless the Lord, O my soul, and forget not all His benefits." If you read this entire psalm, you'll be glad you did. David reminds us that we must keep ourselves in remembrance of what God has done for us. Sometimes, what helps us the most when facing challenging circumstances is being able to look back at all we've already overcome.

Psalm 100 is known as the Psalm of thanksgiving, there are only five verses, but they are very powerful. Verse 3 states, "Know that the Lord, He is God; it is He who has made us, and not we ourselves; we are His people, and the sheep of His pasture." The next time you are aware of being in a lowly state, remember that God is ever present with you, you are his people and he is your God and he inhabits the praises of his people.

About the Author

Latrivette Williams is happily married to Andre Williams Sr. She has one daughter, ShaCorie Cockrell and two step-children, Kiyana Williams and Andre Williams Jr. She is a minster of the gospel. Among being an author, she is a life coach. She coach her clients to live their best life. She enjoy spending time with her family, meeting new people, traveling, and reading. She is devoted to impacting as many lives as she possibly can. For information on her coaching program, email her at push2begin@yahoo.com.

CPSIA information can be obtained
at www.ICGtesting.com
Printed in the USA
LVHW090429200819
628263LV00003B/476/P